SINGING
for the self-conscious

Becky Gilhespie
2 Wharf Road
Berry
NSW 2535
Australia

https://vocals.beckygilhespie.com

This book is dedicated to some special teachers in my life - the ones who saw something in me, and allowed me to shine. Thank you, Leon Berrangé, John Henny, Line Hilton and Leonie Laukkannen.

I want to thank my mom for enrolling me in piano lessons when I was a little girl. That first step into music paved the way for me eventually finding this career path.

And thank you to my amazing friend, IT Helpdesk, Marketing Manager, all-round general supporter and husband, Rogan Gilhespie.

In remembrance of Leona Morgan and Dr. James Edward McCracken, II

How to use this book

This book is full of practical exercises designed to help bring us out of our self-conscious mind so that we can remain in the present moment, have more confidence and authenticity, open up our innate musical creativity, connect more to our material and, therefore, have the ability to deliver it with confidence.

As well as understanding the cognitive elements of self-consciousness, I find it is exercises – the *doing and experiencing* – that can really deliver change over time, and I've written the book with this in mind. The repetition of these exercises is absolutely necessary to make an impact. In guiding students during my 20 years of experience as a vocal coach, I have seen practical exercises deliver profound improvements. I'm confident that when you follow and repeat them often, you will drastically reduce your own self-consciousness.

I've also written this book with a goals focus; that is, the concepts and exercises follow the acronym S.M.A.R.T. (Specific, Measurable, Achievable, Realistic and Time-Bound).

Time to complete: In order to complete this as a 30-day program, aim to spend roughly 10 days on each of the 3 main sections. If you complete the work earlier, repeat the concepts and exercises until it is time to move on to the next section.

Buddy System: What works to achieve even faster, more dramatic results is to do this program with a buddy! You can be supportive, provide feedback to each other, give reassurance and keep each other accountable.

Mailing List: As a special bonus for all my readers, when you join my mailing list, I will send you free training videos to go along with this program to kickstart your singing. confidence! You will also be the first to know about the online course for this program, and receive discounts on all future training with me.

Join Here Now:
https://vocals.beckygilhespie.com/subscribe

Facebook Group: There is a dedicated group on Facebook for people who have purchased this book or online course. Click through here to <u>Singing for Myself</u> (or search FB for "Singing for Myself") and ask to join. This is a space where we can celebrate our wins, have discussions about our biggest blocks and test out the waters singing in front of like-minded people in a safe and supportive environment.

➡ If you like this book and find it helpful, please kindly give it a review on Amazon. This will help others find it.

I have identified a step process which I believe to be a powerful and effective pathway to eliminate debilitating self-consciousness when singing and performing. Each step makes up a chapter in this book.

Of course, there is no quick fix for anything such as this (and never be tempted by any teacher or program who tries to tell you there is). This is going to take awareness, repetition and continual steps forward, but when undertaken in earnest, I'm confident these 8 steps are going to propel you forward with your singing.

So, let's begin. The first step is to read and sign the following 30-day Doing Declaration. Read the text out loud. This is non-negotiable and important!

30-DAY DOING DECLARATION

I,

declare that I am the creator of my own thoughts and actions. Therefore, I choose to move forwards through my fear. I promise myself that I will take at least 30 days to commit to the exercises and activities in this book/program. I promise myself that I will take small action steps everyday to allow my true self to come through when I sing.

SINGING
for the
self-conscious

Becky Gillespie

Section 1: Your Sense of Self

(Steps 1 & 2)

Step 1: Awareness and Acceptance of Self

You know those guys that just bring out their guitars at the party and sing like it's no big deal? Yeah, I've never been that person. Or even the people who just sing out loud in front of other people whenever they get the urge. I just end up cringing and shrivelling. They make it look so easy!

Throughout my singing career, I have only ever sung a few times out loud to my own family. In fact, it's so much easier for me to sing in front of complete strangers. There are so many moments I truly regret holding back. I would've liked to sing at the funerals of my dad and my grandmother, but I chickened out, letting my self-conscious side take over. It is such a shame, because I remember so clearly being three years old and constantly running up and down the hallway singing "opera" into a hairbrush microphone. I was always putting on shows – singing with wild abandon. What happened to that little girl?

If the title of this book popped out at you, I can almost guarantee that you may have had a similar experience. Sometime, during our development, some kind of filter popped into our minds, constantly following us around and muting our chances at self-expression. Holding us back. But what exactly is that filter, anyway?

The fact that you are drawn to singing and music in the first place means that you are the type of person who may be prone to feeling overly self-conscious. Singers are, by their very nature, expressive, intuitive, sensitive and articulate people. It is this artistic nature that could potentially lean towards becoming overly sensitive, causing issues with our confidence or creating unnecessary worries with how we are being perceived. However, we don't need to be governed by this; through awareness, we can even learn to use our artistic traits to our advantage to be more authentic.

What is Self-Consciousness and Where Does it Come From?

Definition

Self-consciousness is a heightened sense of self-awareness. It is a preoccupation with oneself, as opposed to the philosophical state of self-awareness, which is the awareness that one exists as an individual being, though the two terms are commonly used interchangeably or synonymously.

Impairment

When feeling self-conscious, one becomes aware of even the smallest of one's own actions. Such awareness can impair one's ability to perform complex actions. Adolescence is believed to be a time of heightened self-consciousness. A person with a chronic tendency toward self-consciousness may be shy or introverted.

Psychology

Unlike self-awareness, which in a philosophical context is being conscious of one's self as an individual, self-consciousness is being excessively conscious of one's appearance or manner, which can be a problem at times. Self-consciousness is often associated with shyness and embarrassment, in which case a lack of pride and low self-esteem can result. In a positive context, self-consciousness may affect the development of identity, for it is during periods of high self-consciousness that people come the closest to knowing themselves objectively. Self-consciousness affects people in varying degrees, as some people are constantly self-monitoring or self-involved, while others are completely oblivious about themselves.

Psychologists frequently distinguish between two kinds of self-consciousness: private and public. Private self-consciousness is a tendency to introspect and examine one's inner self and feelings. Public self-consciousness is an awareness of the self as it is viewed by others. This kind of self-consciousness can result in self-monitoring and social anxiety. Both private and public self-consciousness are viewed as personality traits that are relatively stable over time, but they are not correlated. Just because an individual is high on one dimension doesn't mean that he or she is high on the other.[1]

It is very common to experience feeling self-conscious when singing in particular. This likely stems from experiencing some form of shame or embarrassment around singing during early childhood experiences. It could be as simple as a singing teacher once casually saying to a student "you don't have much range" or "that doesn't sound good" or, likely in the early years, one of your parents or siblings snickering at you when you were performing your favourite song. It could also be from quite an exposing and humiliating situation, such as from bullying in the school yard. There are so many opportunities for our ego to become bruised and to put up a "safety net" as a result, which can present itself as being self-conscious. It is your mind's way of protecting itself from further damage.

> ❝ To be yourself in a world that is constantly trying to make you something else is the greatest accomplishment." – Ralph Waldo Emerson

Self-Awareness vs. Self-Consciousness

I think it is important to distinguish between the idea of being self-conscious and being self-aware. Awareness of our actions is a good thing, right? We don't want to be one of these people who act out and pay no regard to how their actions affect others. Sort of like when someone has too much to drink and they make a scene.

If you are prone to self-consciousness, then that likely means that you are the type of person who is empathic and sensitive to others' needs, as well as your own. You are not the type of person to just blurt something out without first thinking of the impact it might have, and you are likely a warm, friendly and humble person. You understand what it feels like to be vulnerable, you may have heightened awareness and empathy for others and experience strong emotions . These are parts of your personality which should be <u>celebrated</u>. You can use all of this in your creativity and artistry, channelling these aspects of yourself into captivating, authentic performances.

The songs you sing and love might also reflect these aspects of you. Author Sarah Wilson says she loves the song "I Feel it All" by Feist, because she does (feel it all). I can completely relate.

We just want to take that overly self-conscious part that makes us feel uncomfortable and dull it down.

❝ We need to urgently start to accept and appreciate sensitivity for the temperature regulating effect it has on an often hot-headed world." - Elena Herdieckerhoff, Sensitivity Expert

Corina Pall from International Coach Academy states, "For a person who is self-conscious, the focus of attention gets 'stuck' on herself, i.e. self-consciousness mode; in those moments you want to be able to pay attention to the topic and be completely involved in the conversation, instead you are detached from yourself by being too locked up 'in your head'. Unlike most other people, whose focus is outward, for the self-conscious person, their focus is inward." Self-awareness, on the other hand, keeps us grounded and with the ability to keep our focus on what we are doing in the present moment, without becoming overly preoccupied with internal struggles.

Pall goes on to say that, "Self-awareness is having a clear perception of your personality including strengths, weaknesses, thoughts, beliefs, and emotions. Self-awareness allows you to understand other people, how they perceive you, your attitude and your responses to them in the moment. Self-awareness is the first step in creating what you want. Where you focus your attention, your emotions, reactions, personality and behaviour determine where you go in life."

Self-awareness is positive and necessary for growth. It can be thought of in the same way people use the term "mindfulness", and can be utilized not only to ground us in the present moment, but as a tool of reflection and checking in with ourselves to make the best choices and decisions.

How Do We Encourage Positive Self-Awareness?

Here are 6 ways:

1. **Focus on your breathing:**
    This is a meditation technique that helps us switch off from the brain's preoccupation with other factors. Just a few minutes a day can offer some relief.

2. **Be kind to yourself:**
    Make sure to observe any negative thoughts that come up and try to change them to a more positive concept. For example, changing the thought "That high note sounds awful!" to "I need to work more on this area in my range."

3. **Discover what is making you feel self-conscious:**
Highlight what triggers you have that bring about the feeling of self-consciousness. Challenge your thoughts or make some plans to improve in these areas.

4. **Realise:**
Come to a realisation that as much as it feels people are focussing on you, they really are just consumed with their own reality.

5. **Keep things fun:**
Practice laughing at yourself in a humble way and enjoy each moment - not worrying about what the world might say about you.

6. **Focus on the process rather than the outcome:**
It's ok to still be at the learning stage. Acknowledge that things aren't perfect yet, and that is ok! You'll get there.

By understanding the concepts and completing the exercises in this book through practice/repetition, we can move past being overly self-conscious when singing, while remaining self-aware.

Now let's take a closer look at our troublesome self-consciousness.

How Does Your Self-Consciousness Manifest Itself?

There are a few coping mechanisms that we often take on board when feeling overly self-conscious. I'm sure you can relate to many of these. I'm a self-sabotager and an excessive worrier. Can you pinpoint which of these you do?

1. **Avoidance**

    Turning a blind eye to what we need to do in order to move forward. This can include turning down singing opportunities.

2. **Self-sabotage**

    This happens when we alter the decisions we make in order to avoid feeling self-conscious. This can lead to a lot of missed opportunities and even a totally different life path.

3. **Holding back**

    Not giving your full or true self in any moment due to feeling self-conscious.

4. **Confusion / fluster**

    It's often hard to think/act clearly and logically when a bout of self-consciousness occurs.

5. **Excessive worrying**

   Self-consciousness will mean that you will be worried about how you are perceived by your audience and may bring about lots of unnecessary anxiety.

One can see that these coping mechanisms can get in the way of our rational thought and decision-making processes, potentially making us miss out on opportunities and advancement in life. So, ultimately, our lives are being controlled by our self-consciousness. I am sure you will agree that this is not right and must be stopped.

What If I Hate the Sound of My Own Voice?

Just a note that this is a very common phenomenon. It stems from basically (1) confusion with what you hear coming out of your body and what you feel on the inside, and (2) the age-old concept of "the grass is always greener".

When we vocalise, we experience vibrations through our chest, throat, and nasal cavities. These feelings don't quite line up with the sound that we hear as input through our ears. This can sometimes create a feeling of discordance. This, combined with cultural factors such as accent and our sense of self, means we can experience our own voice negatively and determine that we don't like it.

Perhaps you hear someone else's voice that is totally different to your own – much lighter in timbre or darker in tone - and on hearing the contrast to our own voice, we wish for a voice more like that. This is very common and it takes the experience of regular vocalising and repetition of hearing one's own voice recorded to begin to appreciate it.

Your voice is a part of you. Just accepting that will help. There are certain ways you can improve aspects you may not like but your voice is unique to you and that is a special thing. Believe it!

★Action Step: "Do I accept my voice?"

Once you do make that mental switch to accepting your own voice, it can open up a lot of progression and movement forward. Suddenly, you'll want to nurture and take care of your voice and put time and effort into putting it out there. So, it is worth asking yourself the question: "Do I accept my voice?" If the answer is no, what would it take for you to accept it? Write your answers down.

Self-Expression

Singing is a very pure form of self-expression. It's nice to pause and remember this simple fact. To sing is to release the feelings that are held inside of us. It's too easy to forget this when we sing for other reasons like to try and impress others, or for performances, for example. We can get bogged down in thinking about all the other elements going on. To remember why we sing in the first place and connect how we feel with letting our voice sing out can be very pleasing and truly therapeutic.

❝ Let yourself be drawn by the stronger pull of that which you truly love." – Rumi

Being Authentically You

When you marry aspects of your personality with the way you use your voice, you can feel and come across authentically. It is very powerful and fulfilling to align your sense of self with your voice and expression. In order to do this, you must first get to know yourself.

| Exercise: Who Are YOU? |

Go through the following questions and write them down.
Aim to answer as you truly are, not who you want to be.

What is important to me? Who is important to me?

What are my 3 main values*?

What do I like to do for fun?

Is my heritage important to me? If so, what is it?

How do I identify? (gender, race, age, political stance, romantic status, family, anything that is important to you)

What are my best memories? What were their impacts on me?

What are my worst memories? What were their impacts on me?

What gives me comfort?

What do I dislike?

Am I an introvert or an extrovert? Am I more energized being around others, or by myself?

What am I passionate about?

What makes/made me angry?

What is/was painful to me?

What do I love about my voice?

Why do I sing?

*If you want to explore more about what your key values might be, Brené Brown has made a list of values available online from her book, Dare to Lead. Go through the list and pick the top three that represent what you stand for and believe to be most important to you. There may be many values that you resonate with, but only 2-3 will truly guide your decisions, actions and behaviours (Brown 2018)

The PDF on values can be found here: https://daretolead.brenebrown.com/wp-content/uploads/2019/02/Values.pdf

❝ There is nothing to be self-conscious about when you are being genuine. Enjoy being you!" - Wendy Parr

| Exercise: Singing to Your Soul |

A great first step in becoming a less self-conscious singer is to simply do more singing. Choose a few songs that really speak to your soul. Ones that express how you are feeling, in this current moment, or on this day. By doing this, we are making a conscious effort to bypass fear and bring our true selves to the surface. This way, we release what needs to be expressed.

Here are some ways you could try singing your songs:

1. Find a quiet space at home or in a safe space where you are totally alone. You don't want to worry about anyone listening in. Sing your song, out loud! Simply get used to hearing yourself sing, out loud.

2. Sing in the car. When you pull up to a traffic light, test out not stopping or reducing the intensity of what you are doing, even though you might be afraid other people will see you.

3. Sing in the shower when your family members might be around in the next room and could potentially overhear. Don't feel the need to put

on a funny voice; test out really singing from your heart.

Extra Credit Challenge: Sing one of your favourite songs, out loud, somewhere outside! Film it and upload it to our supportive Facebook group Singing for Myself.

Don't Forget the Lyrics

So often we can be singing a song – something that we have known for years -then all of a sudden realise that we have never even paid any attention to the lyrics or what they mean. Has that ever happened to you? It certainly has to me. One example that comes to mind is 'Fairy Tale of New York' by The Pogues and Kirsty MacColl. Each year in the lead up to Christmas, people merrily sing along to this, completely unaware how tragic the song's storyline is. The first time I actually stopped to contemplate the lyrics and was aware of the song's true meaning, I had to pull my car over and cry. It's a story of Irish immigrants coming to America with a sense of excitement and wonder of possibility, falling in young, crazy love... and then the sobering reality sets in of growing older in poverty, in a stale, resentful relationship under life's insurmountable pressures. And I loved that song a million times more after that – because I connected to the story, heard the truth of it, and the words truly move me every time I hear it now.

Connecting to the lyrics is one way we can bring our awareness into the present moment and distract from a focus on our insecurities. When we connect to the lyrics, our audience also becomes more at ease and they let us take them on a journey.

If you feel slightly disconnected from the songs you sing, try paraphrasing the lyrics in the exercise below so that they pertain to you.

| Exercise: Paraphrasing Your Lyrics |

Pick a song that expresses how you feel today. Write out or print the lyrics, making sure there are spaces for you to write your own notes. Take each phrase and paraphrase it with an experience you may have had, and perhaps make a note about how the phrase or experience makes you feel. Make a note of the underlying feelings, too. Don't think too hard about this, just let the feeling come to mind and write it down.

See my example, below:

"Blowin' In The Wind" by Bob Dylan

How many roads must a man walk down
Before you call him a man?
PARAPHRASE: How long am I going to feel overly self-conscious, Can't I get over this already?
FEELING: (frustration)

How many seas must a white dove sail
Before she sleeps in the sand?
PARAPHRASE: I'm older and tired of this feeling. I just want to be me.
FEELING: (defeated)

Yes, and how many times must the cannonballs fly
Before they're forever banned?
PARAPHRASE: I'm tired of comparing myself to others and feeling not good enough FEELING: (fear)

The answer, my friend, is blowin' in the wind
The answer is blowin' in the wind
PARAPHRASE: The change is within myself and will happen when I allow it.
FEELING: (relief, hope, let it go)

The purpose of this exercise is to let your true feelings come to the surface when you sing. You don't need to worry about acting out the feelings with expressions or gestures (although this may happen naturally).

Simply notice how it changes the way your tone of voice comes across, how it changes the way you phrase the lyrics, how it changes how loud you sing and how you connect with the song.

You may want to move on now to the next section, but I urge you to come back to this exercise and eventually do this for every song in your repertoire. This can be not only a great way of bringing out your true expression when you perform, but also a great way of uncovering and releasing trapped emotion.

You Are Perfectly Imperfect

We are all here in our current, present moment, a collection of all of our experiences to date. We can't be more than we are – we simply are what we are right now, and this is the truth. There is nothing wrong with being you in this very moment, with some imperfections and flaws, and no other person is better than you; it just is how it is. We are all "perfectly imperfect".

It is not to say that you won't get better at certain things in the future, but it can really help with self-acceptance to own this idea, that what's now is now, and that is 100% okay. In fact, these imperfections are what give us interest and depth and connects us to our very human nature. My first singing teacher, Leon, pointed out to me that flaws in live performance are partly what make them so great. Who wants to hear a perfect performance, the exact same as on the recording? No, we want to experience a real, human person, connecting with their art form and expressing that to us. This is what moves us.

★ Listening exercise:

Think of one of your favourite artists and look up a recording or video of him/her performing live. What differences do you notice from the recorded version?

I watched a live performance of Billie Eilish singing "When the Party's Over". I noticed a lot of differences with the breath control and reaching notes (the song is incredibly low and high!) in her live performance, but the imperfections totally added to the experience of singing live. I actually enjoyed the performance more because it wasn't an identical, perfect portrayal of the recorded version.

Comparison – The Thief of Joy

Comparison is such a common problem for singers. We hear or see others sounding amazing and doing fantastic things, and we get a glimpse of envy or start feeling not good enough ourselves. What helps me in moments like these is to turn around those thoughts to feeling happy for that person. I try and think this way especially if it is a friend or colleague of mine. What they are doing says nothing about myself or my situation. In fact, if ever you get a strong negative feeling about something, it can be an important teacher for you. When we are emotionally affected by something in a negative way, it's because there is an insecurity within ourselves that has been triggered. So, that trigger can let us know what areas we are feeling under-confident in, and we can then work on that.

When I get those negative feelings that stem from comparison or feeling envy/not good enough, I take a moment to pause and notice the negative thoughts (without any judgement on myself), and then I express gratitude for the ability to learn things from that person and their performance, or for the great musical experience I just had.

** That chick right there has paved the way for me and a lot of other sisters, and I appreciate it. We all have our own thing, and that's the magic. Everybody comes with their own sense of strength and their own queendom. Mine could never compare to hers, and hers could never compare to mine." Artist Jill Scott, talking about Erykah Badu

★ Action Step: **Express Gratitude**

Inducing feelings of gratitude can simply bring our mindset from a negative focus into positive. Done daily, this is a powerful exercise in shifting our thoughts and feelings. This can also be done anywhere, on the go and in seconds.

Press the fingers of one hand to your sternum, close your eyes (if safe to do so) and breathe a few slow, deep breaths. Bring to mind *anything* that you feel grateful for in your life and in your present moment. This can be a person, a situation, a silver lining, or something quite ordinary, such as the wind blowing through the trees, the snap of good quality chocolate, or hanging laundry in the sun.

Remember that your voice is totally unique. If everyone sounded the same then music would be extremely boring! And when I refer to your unique voice, I mean not only what you sound like, but what you have to say and bring to the world. You are your own collection of unique experiences and world views that no one else in the world has. This is what makes us unique and different, and also interesting to others.

Not Always as it Seems

People have often said to me that I seem very confident and relaxed. Wow, if only they could see inside my whirlwind of a mind! It is amazing how we can come across differently to how we feel on the inside.

Often, what we see is not actually the reality. In this age of perfect Instagram photos, it's easy to forget that everyone is not as perfect as they seem and get swept up in comparison. I have worked with several high-profile celebrities and singers, and I'm always pleasantly surprised at how normal they are in real life. They are human beings, just like me, with flaws and imperfections.

I recently watched a live solo gig of Coldplay's lead singer Chris Martin. He was making a joke of the fact that he felt nervous, and he even admitted to not remembering many of his song lyrics. This was so refreshing to see such a big name singer admitting these things. Instantly, he seemed very authentic to me, and I related to him as a result of this.

Instead of completely hiding your self-consciousness, pretending you don't feel a certain way, why not expose them and use these feelings to your advantage? People want to know that the singer they are listening to is real and authentic – not putting on an act. When you chat with an audience before and during a performance, you get a chance to connect with them. You can go ahead and "blurt out" that you may be feeling nervous, anxious or even scared. You will be surprised at the reaction, especially if you smile and/or laugh. It truly is endearing, and not only will it help your audience connect with you, but it will also help your own feelings and nervous energy to be released.

> **"** Always be a first-rate version of yourself and not a second-rate version of somebody else." – Judy Garland

Let Your Light Shine

I love how every singing voice is unique. No other person in the world will ever sound like you do. There is no other instrument in the world like yours. And yes, your voice is an instrument!

With singing and music, we are able to use our instrument together with our self-expression. I think this is one of the reasons why it can make us feel so exposed. Because when we sing, we are being vulnerable and open, but there is true beauty and authenticity in this! People respect and, therefore, connect with true vulnerability.

When we experience a singer "letting go", it is truly mesmerising. This is because it touches something within our own sense of self. We are witnessing another human-being "show" his/her true self and this is powerful. We recognise this to be a special moment and we appreciate the vulnerability it took to expose this truth.

In order to open ourselves to others, we must overcome our fear. Here is a wonderful excerpt from Leonie Laukkannen's, book, "Mother Om":

> ❝ In moments of intense darkness, we see elements of our soul that lead us to discover our truth. So many of us live in our darkness and we use our fear like a heavy curtain to block out the light. In a room full of darkness, we can always see the light, shining through the cracks. If we embrace our light, the light grows and the darkness fades. We all have a light inside us. I'm not afraid of my darkness anymore. In fact, there have been times

that I have been more afraid of my light. It shines like a diamond and it's overwhelmingly beautiful. Our darkness makes us appreciate our light and our light gives us gratitude for our darkness."

– Leonie (Percy) Laukkannen

To be overly self-conscious is to be acting from a state of fear but, ultimately, this is a choice (even if it often doesn't feel like that in the middle of an overly self-conscious experience). We can *choose* to be able to dance like nobody's watching or sing like no one is listening! We can *choose* to dull down that aspect of our personality that holds us back and let our true nature shine through.

Notes from Step 1: Awareness and Acceptance of Self

Step 2: Eliminate Negative Mindset Patterns

Our mindset has a powerful grip on literally everything we do. After my research, I believe it is almost impossible to move forward until we address underlying patterns and beliefs which may be subconsciously sabotaging our best intentions.

The Powerful Subconscious Mind

Image credit: PSYCH-K

This diagram shows how the makeup of our consciousness is relatable to an iceberg, in that we carry out our conscious, day to day awareness, thinking and actions with only 10% of our cognition – this is like the tip of the iceberg that is shown on the surface. A whopping 90% of our mind's functioning operates at the sub-conscious level.

We can think of our subconscious mind as a large, automated storage vault for everything ever experienced. (InnerJam 2020). Our subconscious mind stores information it receives about our relationship with the external world, writes up an "operating program", and then acts in accordance with this programming. So even if we are thinking a certain way, and attempting to take a specific action, our subconscious mind often conflicts with this, and works in accordance to its' original operating programming. We are usually totally unaware of this as it happens in each moment, since the programming resides in our subconscious mind.

The good news is that we can actually "re-wire" our programming. This takes awareness and then action, in order to change the way we typically react to situations. This is something you are doing right now by reading this book. You have awareness that your self-consciousness is not coming from your logical, present, action-taking mind. No, it is stemming from fears lying underneath the surface. And it is getting in your way.

Mindfulness is a great way to start the process of having more awareness about our sub-conscious programming. to our conscious decision making. Mindfulness is simply listening to our thoughts, noticing them without judgement or reaction. When we notice our thoughts, and choose not to react, then we are sending a message to our sub-conscious mind to change the programming.

| Exercise: Journaling and Meditating on Your Thoughts

1.   Imagine yourself about to perform. Grab a pen and paper and start writing down all the thoughts you are having, no matter how silly or abstract they are. Ask yourself the question: "What *exactly* am I worried about?"

2.   Close your eyes, reflect on these thoughts and ask yourself the following two questions: "<u>Are they useful?</u>" and "<u>How do they behave?</u>"

Note: These particular questions are actual translations from the ancient language of Sanskrit and are still used to silence an overactive, negative mind. It works! You can use these questions any time you have a busy mind filled with worry. You can watch a TED talk on this subject by Anthony Metivier.

3.   Try a meditation mantra: Breathe slowly and deeply, in and out (this signals to your brain and nervous system

that you are okay). Choose a short mantra to repeat during your breathing exercise. My favourite is: "I'm breathing in strength; I'm breathing out negativity." I like to envision breathing in crystal clear, white light and breathing out stale, grey air (but you may see it differently). Keep returning to this mantra. It doesn't matter if your mind is busy (totally normal). Just keep gently guiding it back to the mantra.

4.   Now, daydream about yourself having the best ever performance. Really go into detail and see yourself nailing it. Go through the lyrics of your songs and see/hear yourself singing the big notes or complicated parts of the material.

Return to these exercises whenever you need, but aim to do at least one per day – in the morning before getting up or in the evening just before bedtime is the most powerful time to meditate and calmly reflect.

Growth vs Fixed Mindset

Having a growth mindset (the belief that you are in control of your own ability and will learn and improve) is also key to advancement and development in any area you wish to improve. Yes, hard work, effort, and persistence are all important, but not as important as feeling and knowing that *you are in control* of your own destiny.

One of the most basic beliefs we carry about ourselves, Stanford Psychologist Carol Dweck found in her research, has to do with how we view and inhabit what we consider to be our personality. A "fixed mindset" assumes that our character, intelligence, and creative ability are static givens which we can't change in any meaningful way. A "growth mindset," on the other hand, thrives on challenge and sees failure not as evidence of unintelligence but as a possibility for growth and for stretching our existing abilities. A great deal of our behaviour, our relationship with success and failure in both professional and personal contexts, and ultimately our capacity for happiness, has its roots in either of these two mindsets. (Popova 2014)

The following image shows some perspectives from both fixed and growth mindsets:

Image credit: Ideapod 2019

Healing Unconscious Damage with Conscious Attention

Psychoanalysis was founded by Dr Sigmund Freud following his discovery that his patients could be cured when the unconscious factors underlying their issues, whether repressed memories or emotions, were brought forward to the conscious mind. Many followers of psychoanalysis believed, however, that changes were only made possible when carried out by a trained professional. But Keren Horney was a leading psychoanalyst who believed that it could be carried out alone. She called it "Self-Analysis", and thought it possible to be even more effective than traditional therapy. Afterall, we already know ourselves inside and out, whereas a therapist is starting from scratch with a complete stranger to learn the inner workings and complexities of a patient. (Academy of Ideas 2018) Horney also believed that every human is on a natural path towards growth and self-realization, but unfortunately most people's journey towards realization is interrupted due to forms of childhood trauma. (Horney 51)

Line Hilton is one of my long-term singing coaches who specialises in Performing Arts Medicine (similar to sports medicine but for the arts) which addresses performance-related, or caused, problems and performance-affecting problems. While writing the mindset section of this book, I sought help from Line, who opened my eyes to how our underlying beliefs remain at the heart of nearly every decision we make.

Our Limiting Self-Beliefs

We create our beliefs at an early age based on our life experiences and perceptions of the world around us. "Beliefs are internal commands to the brain to represent what is happening, when we believe something to be true." (Roa, Asha and Vasudeveraju 2010) We create many beliefs in our early years during the fragile development of our sense of self, and this is commonly when negative self-beliefs begin to form.

Let's take a look at some very common negative self-beliefs. Read through the following list and see if any of these statements resonate with you. You won't have to think too hard - you will know, just by reading the statement and feeling a twinge, a tension, or a pull of some sort.

I'm not good enough
I'm not worthy
Mistakes and failure are bad
I'm not talented
I'm a faker/fraud
I'm a disappointment
I'm not deserving
I'll never get what I want
My needs are not important
I'm powerless
I'm bad
If I make a mistake, I'll be rejected
What makes me good enough is doing things perfectly

These self-beliefs come from our developmental stage, before the age of 7, when we are constantly gathering information from the world around us for our own self-development. Often, we experience a negative response from a parent or carer. For example, a parent angrily snaps at a little boy when he tries to help with giving the baby a bath. In that moment, he forms a negative self-belief that he is bad and that if he makes mistakes, he will be rejected. The actions that form a limiting self-belief can range from an angry glance to, at the other end of the spectrum, physical or mental abuse. Interestingly, Line also states that limiting self-beliefs can even form from too much *positive* feedback as a child. For example, always receiving praise and never being told that a child must adjust and correct mistakes is not as it is in the real world. This can result in a self-belief of being a fraud or phony, or having to be perfect all the time.

So, our negative self-beliefs can really shape our life and be a constant underlying theme in the decisions we make. However, the key thing to remember is that *WE are the creators* of our beliefs. Sure, the event that happened came from our parent/carer which became the catalyst to our deciding that we aren't good enough, or we aren't worthy, but WE ourselves created that belief.

" If you accept a limiting belief, it will become your truth." – Louise Hay

So, as the creator of our own negative self-beliefs, *we* are the only ones who can change this.

| Exercise: Alternative Interpretation |

1. Take one or more of the limiting self-beliefs that you have from the list above and write them down below:

_____

_____

2. Can you recall a life situation where this self-belief got in the way? If you are unsure, pick an instance where you simply felt very uncomfortable and had an adverse reaction of some sort to an event that happened.

For example: A colleague made a negative comment after a presentation you gave at work. You then felt hurt and hung onto this comment in your mind and couldn't let it go. Finally, you concluded that the presentation was terrible and you never showed it to anyone ever again. You had the underlying feeling of "<u>I'm not good enough</u>".

Write down your particular personal situation(s) below:

_____

_____

_____

3. Think about this situation and how it ended. Now write down 3 *other* possible likely interpretations that could've been true for this situation.

For example: A. The colleague who gave feedback was biased and didn't like this particular project for a random reason which had nothing to do with your performance. B. The colleague was having an off day and was in a bad mood, and their words didn't come out sensitively. C. The comment had some truth to it, but it was about an area that you may need to work on. You are an expert, however, in other areas.

You see, we create meaning and conclusions around the events that happen to us, but these conclusions aren't necessarily the actual truth for the situation. This is merely *our interpretation* of the event, and we have created a meaning behind it. We then live our lives with this meaning attached. Every time something similar happens we then tell ourselves "Mistakes and failure are bad" or "I'm not good enough", for example.

I want you to take your own life situation example(s) and then write down 3 alternative possibilities that could have been true, other than the conclusion that you came to. Write those alternative interpretations below:

_____

_____

_____

It's a powerful thing when we realise that we ourselves make assumptions based on outcomes of life events. These assumptions cause us to form limiting self-beliefs. Our assumptions are most likely WRONG, but they end up staying with us for a lifetime, repeating the same patterns over and over.

★Action step: The Lefkoe Method

I would like you to now complete an exercise which is all about uncovering, understanding and then changing our limiting self-beliefs. To access this powerful, life changing exercise, visit *https://www.mortylefkoe.com* and subscribe. When you subscribe to their mailing list, you will watch a powerful video which will take you through the process of changing a negative self-belief in about 20 minutes.

This process claims to eradicate your negative self-belief, forever!

Our Mean Thoughts

Often, when we are feeling overly self-conscious or overwhelmed, we can't even put a finger on what it actually is; we just feel terrible. This often plays out in a kind of anxious, nervous energy. Sound familiar?

For me, I tend to get hundreds of thoughts whirring around in my head, and none of them stop long enough for me to get a clear look into it. Each one swings by and quickly says something mean to me, and then heads off to make room for the next mean thought to take its turn.

I now know that these kinds of quick-fire, whirring thoughts are just part of an anxious pattern of thinking. The majority of them have no real meaning or weight behind it – it literally is just a mean thought! These thoughts stem from our subconscious brain and are there because of some kind of past trauma. Remember, as singing is a form of expressing ourselves, we can often feel quite exposed and vulnerable, which brings past wounds to the surface.

❝ Take small steps every day and you WILL get there." – Unknown

Literally almost every performer has some kind of past experience with someone telling them they didn't like their singing, or even their laughing. These experiences have resulted in a severely bruised ego and often are at the heart of the reason people declare "I can't sing". It can be so hard to let go of this which, by the way, is totally untrue. Everyone can sing! It is our mind and subconscious fear that get in the way and stop us from believing in ourselves. The good news is that if we can identify our mean thoughts and see them for their ugly truths, they can be cast aside like the bullies they are.

| Exercise: Exposing Your Mean Thoughts |

For this exercise, you'll need someone close to you; someone you know well and trust.

1. Sing a song or part of a song out loud, as if it were a performance. During your performance, make a note of all the thoughts coming into your head. (When I did this exercise, I had things written down such as "Your high notes sound terrible" and even "You're ugly and fat"!)

2. Now, write down your thoughts on a piece of paper and hand them to your friend.

3. Proceed to sing again, and this time have your friend read those thoughts out loud to you as you sing.

So mean, right? We would never say these things to a friend, yet we say it to ourselves all the time. And remember that these types of thoughts have no real truth behind them. They are not true!

4. Have a conversation with your friend to get feedback on this.

Now that you have exposed these particular mean thoughts, you have a new awareness of them. So, the next time you are singing and notice these thoughts creeping in, you will know that they are just the bullies in your mind, fuelled by insecurity. They are not real!

Case Study: Self-Conscious Singers in the Public Eye

The following famous singers have been out-spoken with their internal battles when it comes to singing and performing:

1. **Cher**: She originally could not even sing on stage without her partner, Sonny, and started by looking only at him on stage.

2. **Carly Simon**: Despite being referred to as one of the greatest ever songwriters, she has not done much live work due to suffering from panic attacks and even once collapsing before a show.

3. **Brian Wilson**: The lead singer of the Beach Boys has said that he hated every single show due to a terrible feeling of anxiety and stage fright.

4. **Adele**: Listening to her strong vocals, it is surprising to know that Adele is actually terribly shy and suffers from extreme fear every time she performs live.

5. **Barbra Streisand**: She once forgot some lyrics during a live concert. This led to a bout of severe performance anxiety and a 27-year break from performing live. After this, she refuses to perform without a teleprompter, even for talking in between songs.

Mental Health in Music

Sadly, it is all too common amongst artists and musicians to suffer through a wide variety of mental health issues. It is likely that the reason many suffering people choose music as their outlet is its cathartic nature and the way it helps us to express ourselves. Thus, we see a heavy proportion of people in the music industry who struggle with mental health.

When the situation crosses the blurry lines from being overly self-conscious, to overly anxious, to no longer being able to function properly, it can be wise to seek out professional help. As I mentioned previously, I suffered through anxiety and depression for pretty much the whole of my twenties and hid it from nearly everyone around me, but it wasn't until I sought help and received counselling and therapy that I could get to the root of some internal issues and move forward. This was a tremendous help for me as a singer, as well as being able to function normally in my day to day life.

Just by reaching for this book, you have made the first steps in choosing to let go of crippling self-consciousness. I've been there too. You can overcome this. You are not defined by being an overly self-conscious person.

❝ Everyone has inside them a piece of good news. The good news is you don't know how great you can be! How much you can love. What you can accomplish. And what your potential is." - Anne Frank

| Exercise: Focusing on the Positive |

It is all too easy to get caught up in what we haven't yet achieved or all the things we haven't done right. How about all the things that you have already done? Sometimes when we stop to reflect on all that we have done, we can realise that we have, in fact, achieved a lot. Even just by buying this book/course, you are one step closer to becoming a better, more open and creative singer.

- Reflect on your life and what has brought you to this point. Make a list of 5 (or more) major life events that you have overcome to bring you to this point you're at today.
- List 10 things that you love about yourself.
- List 10 skills that you have.
- List 5 people whom you have helped.

Line Hilton is particularly passionate about the power of our mindset and is a qualified Rapid Transformational Therapist. RTT helps eliminate limiting beliefs, thought patterns and behaviours at the subconscious level. Within RTT sessions, adjustments are made to our subconscious mind, as fears can be deeply rooted within our subconscious mind. To be able to shift things there is very powerful. Since the work is done while hypnotised, RTT sessions are an extremely *fast* way to rid yourself of hindering negative thought patterns and behaviours for good.

Changes are possible in 1-3 sessions, unlike traditional therapy. Line states that her clients have gone on to accomplish amazing things after undertaking RTT and clearing their blocks.

I myself had a session in the run up to releasing this book and online program, as I was experiencing feelings of being not good enough and the fear of rejection. Being hypnotised felt incredible, like I was floating on a cloud and very relaxed, yet my mind remained always clear and in control. During the session my subconscious mind brought forward some instances from my childhood where I had formed negative beliefs based around an event or circumstance. Then, Line walked me through a process of letting these beliefs go, since they no longer serve me as a capable adult. I instantly felt lighter, like nearly a lifetime of negative baggage had been cleared away, and that is exactly what happened! The next day I woke up feeling very positive. Now, at the time of writing this, it is exactly 1 month since my RTT session. I feel like I'm gaining confidence every day and generally feeing more confident in my own skin. I've been able to talk freely about the launch of my book without the fear of rejection or having the feeling of being not good enough.

You can get in touch with Line for more information by contacting her via her website or emailing her. She offers a free consultation call.

Line Hilton
MSc PAM, B.Mus.Ed, C.Hyp,
MHFA | RTT | Wraw Master Practitioner
Social Media @linehilton
W: linehilton.com
 E: info@linehilton.com

Her page on RTT: https://www.linehilton.com/rapid-transformational-therapy-rtt/

Notes from Step 2: Eliminate Negative Mindset Patterns

Section 2: Evolving Your Craft

(Steps 3, 4 & 5)

Step 3: Develop Your Technique

I am primarily a technique teacher. What I mean by that is that when I teach singing, I focus 80% of the lesson time doing exercises, balancing the voice and addressing issues with strain, weak areas and navigating the vocal break. The remaining 20% is usually focussed on rhythm, the syncopation of lyrics and tongue twisters.

I do not *teach* style (although we might discuss some musical genres and compare the way different singers *typically* use their voices in certain styles), and I do not actually teach the topics and ideas covered in this book during private lessons. That is because these things cannot really be taught. They are part of a personal journey we must experience ourselves. So, the topics in this book are meant for a conversation, an awareness and a personal exploration you must undertake yourself. I can't teach anyone to be less self-conscious, but I can help open a dialogue and provide experiences for people to do this work themselves.

I remember taking intensive lessons when I was training to become a vocal coach. I was feeling a little frustrated because my main teachers and mentors were focusing 90% of the time on technique, and while the training was great, I knew in my heart that the thing that was really holding me back as a singer was this crippling self-consciousness. Even though I could nail the majority of the techniques they were giving me (and I'd often get a lot of praise within the lessons) I just felt like a fraud. Sure, I could do "perfect" exercises, but something was holding me back. Something big.

This "thing" was within me. It was a struggle within my own mind, and no one could truly help release it but myself.

That is why I'm writing this book. No, you can't teach someone to let go of their self-consciousness, which is why I teach mainly technique, just like my mentors. However, this is a conversation we can have, which can then spur awareness and start the ball rolling for you to do the work you need to do to let go and, in turn, let your true creativity shine.

Technique Is First

Having a strong technique has got to be the *first* port of call when it comes to working on your singing. It is the same concept as when a runner works on their stride, or trains their legs at the gym to improve stamina and strength. Our vocal cords are made of muscle, after all. Having a trained voice will give many more aspects and possibilities to your voice and that, in turn, gives us less to be self-conscious about. Technique also gives us something to hold on to when we are feeling unstable.

One thing is for sure: If there are technical issues with your voice, this will be the thing that stands out in a performance. Think wobbly notes, straining for high notes and voice breaking. So, this trumps any shyness or hindrances with being overly self-conscious. I think this is also a big reason why my mentors don't teach style. There is a lot to cover usually in technique alone, and working through this would be the first priority in getting a singer to sound better.

" Nothing is particularly hard if it is divided into small jobs." – Henry Ford

What Is the Best Technique?

There are some great techniques out there, and most cover similar aspects of voice, but they can be quite different in the way they see and explain things. Not every technique works for every person. I'm simply going to answer the question about which one is best by saying you should find one that works for you and stick with it. Having a method to follow can give us so much confidence. It gives us tools to use, which, in turn, will help us to feel less self-conscious.

You may have to keep an open mind and try out a few different lessons before you find one that makes an impact. Ask your teacher what technique he/she follows. It should be based on scientific studies and research. A good teacher will have knowledge of vocal anatomy and the physiological requirements to correct a vocal issue, however, he/she might put the instruction in a way that is more helpful to you and your learning style.

Interestingly, a recent study concluded that an external "focus of attention" in voice training can lead to improved skill development and superior performance (The Voice Foundation, 2020). An example of external focus instruction might be to "throw your voice up like a ball" as opposed to a more internally focused instruction of "release to your head voice". For example, accuracy in golf performance went up when players were instructed to focus externally on the trajectory of the ball, instead of internally on the position of their wrists. So, you may receive external instruction from your teacher, and it is always great to feedback and let your teacher know what works for you.

Your voice teacher should be supportive and passionate about you and your goals. You deserve someone who will get behind you and build you up rather than knock you down. Someone with a kind and empathic nature will help you move from strength to strength; NOT an authoritarian style, hard-nosed teacher who makes you feel like your voice lesson is all about her/him. This type of person will only re-enforce any underlying negative self-beliefs you might have and can do a lot of damage in the long run. Stay away from these types!

The technique you are learning should not have one "guru" but rather have input from several experts from the medical community, professional singers and leading voice teachers. Your voice should feel better, more flexible and more free, after following the method. It should be able to give you the results you are after over time, and a main element should be vocal health and care of the voice.

❝ No matter how many mistakes you make or how slow you progress, you're still way ahead of everyone who isn't trying." Tony Robbins

This is not a technique book, as there is simply too much to cover. I will, however, give you a few of the exercises and concepts that I use in my approach of training singers.

The Best Singers Make the Strangest Noises

When singers come into my studio for singing lessons, I can immediately tell roughly how much experience they have. Not by how they sound or what they are wearing, or how much music industry lingo they use. I immediately know how experienced/inexperienced they are by how comfortable they are vocalising during the lesson.

It's actually quite amazing to think that the very first thing we did when we came into this world was make a sound. Our voice is such a key part of who we are, most of us literally vocalise from the moment we wake until the moment we go to sleep, yet we remain feeling only comfortable (stuck) in the few pitches we regularly use for speaking.

Think of an instrumentalist warming up before a show. They must access all the notes, from low to high. If it is a wind instrument, the correct air pressure and mouth position must be practiced and achieved. If it is a string instrument, the correct holding position of the instrument on the body or away from the body, the correct use of the fingers to pluck the strings or use of a bow or plectrum. In other words, they warm up every aspect of usage, which is both auditory and physical. Our voice instrument is no different.

Within the first 5 minutes of a singing lesson (after our initial chat), we get straight down to business exploring the ins and outs of voice production, and I'm not sure if you have noticed, but the very business of singing or speaking involves making noise! The good news is we are born with the natural ability to make a great big sound (think of a baby crying).

Speaking on Pitch

Technically, our singing voice is the same as our spoken voice. We actually speak on pitches, just like in singing, although for speaking it is only 1 or 2 pitches, and in the same part of our range. Singing requires jumping all around, high and low. You can actually find the pitches you use in speech on the keys of a piano. My voice fluctuates around A/Bb below middle C. The only differences in singing and speaking are that we use more pitches when we sing, and we hold notes out for a length of time rather than the clipped manner we vocalise with for speech.

Vowels and Consonants

Vowels and consonants are the main tools we use to speak and sing. They are like our paints, with which we can deliver our lyrics in a way that is vibrant and bold, or soft and subdued.

Consonants: I love the line from Joni Mitchell's song "Big Yellow Taxi": "They paved paradise, and put up a parking lot." Those glorious p's are just meant to create a rhythmical bounce in the delivery of that line.

A great place to start when looking at consonants is with tongue twisters.

| Exercise: Tongue Twisters |

These are crucial for diction, syncopation of lyrics and general mouth movement/energy required for singing. The goal isn't to go as fast as possible, but to feel the rhythm of the prose and to get clarity on each word. Here are a few of my favourite tongue twisters:

- "How much wood would a woodchuck chuck if a woodchuck could chuck wood?"
- "A proper cup of coffee in a proper coffee cup"
- "Brown bears bake bread for breakfast"
- "My mother makes me munch my M&Ms on a Monday morning"
- "The teeth and the tongue and the lips"

" Consonants not only give us understandable language, they are the rhythmic drivers of music, containing a whole world of expressive possibilities." - John Henny, Author of Teaching Contemporary Singing

Vowels: I want to state for the record that vowels are a HUGE factor in singing well. Vowels are literally shapes that we create in our throat and mouth. There are so many different ways of shaping vowels. Just test out, right now, saying "Oh" in several different ways: long vowel, wide vowel, shallow vowel, deep vowel.

Vowels create resonance. I want to say this again in another way because it is key: The choice of vowels you use can create a more *resonant* voice. And, generally speaking, resonance sounds pleasing to our ears.

Technically speaking, more resonance is produced when the sound waves and air pressure coming through our vocal instrument are balanced with each other. This results in boosted frequencies, or harmonics, and as a result a "ringing" quality can be heard. These ringing sounds we hear are the overtones of the fundamental base note (the pitch we hear most prominently), and the frequencies of each resulting overtone are multiplied twice in value.

Are you still with me after that? This is even an amalgamation of the more basic explanations I found in my research. Our vocal instrument is wonderfully intricate and complicated and this is why I could not possibly make this a book about technique as well. If you'd like more information about the anatomy and workings of your voice, I recommend the website voicescienceworks.org.

One of the differences between speech and singing is that we speak in a clipped manner, but when we sing, we hold our notes on the vowel shapes. This is our chance to choose the best possible shape that will create the most impact, and finding the right shape can also make your voice feel at ease and balanced. You may notice a ringing sensation or that vibrato will more naturally occur with the most resonant shape.

| Exercise: Exploring Vowel Shapes |

1.Repeat the sound "YEEEEEEOOOOOEEEEEEE" very slowly, noticing the feeling of the resonance of each changing shape in your mouth and how the resonant feeling moves in a circle around your mouth, from front to back and front again.

2. Let's use 'diphthongs" (vowels that have two or more connected parts) to get our voice moving around the shapes. Repeat very slowly, like a slowed-down recording, the following vowel shapes:

A (Eh-ee), I (Uh-ee), Oh (Uh-oo), Oi (Uh-oo-ee), Ow (Ah-oo)

3. Now let's try the line "And I, will always love you" from Dolly Parton's hit song, or perhaps you know it better from Whitney Houston's cover. First sing without any adjustment. Next, hold the shape of "I" more like an "UH". How did this adjust the sound and feeling of your singing?

Listen to the following female contemporary singers and how different they sound in tone and weight of voice:

1. Kate Bush – light voice and bright tone
2. Adele – full voice and bright tone
3. Tracy Chapman – light/medium weighted voice and dark tone
4. Betty Carter – light voice and dark tone

We don't typically hear "dark" tone very often in contemporary music. It is usually heard more often in classical singing. We can adjust our tone with our vowels and larynx position, which is why I've included this listening example in the technique section, rather than in style, although you can also use tone as a stylistic effect, as well.

| Exercise: Reciting Poetry |

Song lyrics can be similar to poetry, in that the words are written to have a certain diction and rhythm that we can play with when we sing. Pick a piece of poetry and recite it, out loud. Make sure to feel the rhythm of the prose and tell a story in the way you recite the words. Which words do you highlight in each line? For example: "ONCE upon a MIDNIGHT dreary, while I PONDERED, weak and WEARY".

You can be a little exaggerated and theatrical in this exercise. I like to think about reading poetry in the same way you would read a bedtime story to a child. More enthusiastic than your normal reading manner.

Like Having a Cup of Tea

The most experienced of singers are so used to the feeling of using their voice and vocalising through their range, making all kinds of noises, that they no longer feel silly or strange when doing so. Think of an instrumentalist warming up before a rehearsal or gig. It really is no different, but because our instrument is our voice, which is attached to us, I suppose this can create feelings of self-consciousness.

The theory behind the statement "like having a cup of tea" is simple. You want to make an activity as normal and effortless as possible, so it becomes an everyday, mundane thing – like having a cup of tea.

I'll never forget the paralysing fear of Huntsman spiders I felt when we moved to Australia. I simply could not stop thinking about it, and the more I got into a heightened state over anticipating where and when I would see one, the worse it became. I even hallucinated seeing one creeping out of my laundry basket. "Don't worry, Huntsman are the 'Labradors of the spider world,'" I kept getting told, but that comment never seemed to relax me.

Then, we moved into this stunning garden cottage in the leafy Eastern Suburbs of Sydney. This charming, rustic cottage was on the grounds of one of the original historic houses in Sydney originating around 1860. In other words, the doors had no seals, and the original wooden floor boards and intricate iron vents had huge gaps leading to the open air. Needless to say, it wasn't long before huge spiders and other creepy crawlies started showing up in our space. At first, I was stunned and paralysed. I had to call the landlord to come and help me every time this happened. But then – and I'm not even sure how or when this happened - I started to feel a little less afraid when I saw one, and less anxious about the possibility of seeing one.

Spiders became a part of our daily lives in Australia, and I dare say I even started to find Huntsman spiders kind of gangly and cute. To this day, my fear has subsided. I wouldn't want to hold one, but if I do see one up on the wall, I don't have a panic attack.

| Exercise: Making Exaggerated Sounds and Faces |

Make it a part of your daily routine to vocalise, and to make some weird, exaggerated sounds at that. We also must move our mouth and get used to making exaggerated facial expressions (a very natural aspect of singing). I've included some of my favourite vocal exercises. These, when repeated and applied in patterns through your vocal range, truly do increase the muscle tone, flexibility, and extension of your singing voice. Plus, at the same time, we are using our exaggerated sounds and faces, which I've seen and experienced help so many singers with general voice usage.

| Vocal Exercises |

Lip Trill: For this exercise you are going to "bubble" your lips by keeping them relaxed while pushing air through them. Hold your lips to the sides, just underneath them, and blow air through your loose lips so they flap. Aim to make a siren from low to high. Notice the steady flow of air required to maintain the lip trill.

> *Why? Bubbling your lips mimics the action of the vocal cords: closing and vibrating against a natural flow of air. Closing your full voice off at the mouth creates a back pressure, which balances the air above and below the glottis (area of the larynx which contains the vocal cords). The position of the vocal tract here is also the perfectly relaxed and neutral "middle vowel" /ə/ pronounced like "uh" (American English) or "er" (British English) "B(a)nan(a)"*

Trumpet Lips: Puff out your cheeks but keep your lips almost completely shut. Blow air through this position and make sound, on a siren from low to high and back again. This exercise is also great to do in place of song lyrics – especially on difficult areas.

> *Why? Similar to the lip trill, closing the lips creates a back pressure of air which balances the voice and puffing out the cheeks holds the vocal tract in a good position for healthy singing. This is called an S.O.V.T (Semi Occluded Vocal Tract) exercise. This also sets up diaphragmatic breath exhalation for singing.*

Weeee! Wooo! As if you are being pushed on a swing, say "Weeee!" high into your head voice, like a siren. Exclaim "Wooo!" as if you are at a baseball game.

> *Why? The narrow vowels ee and oo help us in singing higher, and the feeling of gliding on a siren helps us to use a flow phonation that is relaxed and not squeezed. We can feel lots of "head resonance" from our upper register here.*

Nagh (Bully): Nagh, as in "CAT". Exclaim "Nagh nagh nagh nagh nagh" in the sing song, very bratty voice that a bully would use.

> *Why? This wide vowel increases adduction (closure) of the vocal cords. This creates more muscle tone, strength and connection to the lower register.*

Nay (Witchy): Use the same bratty quality on the sound "Nay nay nay" and do this on any scale going up through your range.

Why? The diphthong vowel "A" (Ehee) moves from wide to narrow. This, along with the "witchy" quality, assists the voice in carrying less weight in order to make the necessary adjustments to increase in pitch.

Goog (as in 'book'): Add a "sobbing" quality to your voice and repeat on any scale going up through the middle of your range.

Why? The sob or cry quality elongates the vocal folds which helps us sing through the vocal break and into the upper register. The use of the G consonants provide support in vocal cord closure.

Blah Blah Blah: repeat this in a spoken voice, over and over while altering the pitch of your voice. Aim to lengthen your mouth, so that it is more like "Bluh"

Why? This word results in natural, speech-like vocal production and can help with keeping the mind and body relaxed while vocalising.

Looking in a Mirror: Repeat the above exercises while looking in a mirror. Notice the expressions you make on each one, such as lifting your eyebrows or crinkling your eyes. While you are here, go ahead and make some intense facial expressions over and over again and watch yourself. I know this sounds weird, but trust me, this helps in the long run!

Why? This bridges the gap between what you feel in your mind as you do exercises and the reality. It often feels so much more exaggerated in our heads than it looks on the outside.

| Exercise: Marking Out Your Technique |

Before we can get to the styling of our songs, it's best if we sing through every bit and plan out what we are doing technically. Even on a simple song that isn't very challenging, I like to sing through at least twice before I get a feel for what my voice is doing on the notes. I go through, section by section, and repeat lines/phrases as necessary until I know how to approach them. This step is *crucial* to singing confidently.

You will begin to navigate your voice on the notes that lie in your bridge, which notes require a different vowel shape, or which notes require more/less air.

1.   Print your lyrics for each song that you would like to cover.
2.   Sing through each section. You may need to do this acapella (without music), and slowed down so that you can feel each note. Repeat as necessary, and alter your process as required until it feels right on each note.
3.   Make notes on your lyrics as to what you need to do.

4. If you are struggling with some notes, then you can book a session with a vocal coach for help, or perhaps it is a case of practicing more until you get it, or approaching the notes in a different way.

| Exercise: Staying in Focus |

So often when singing, we are subconsciously rushing just to get through. This exercise requires a sharp focus on each phrase of the song, which will make you focus on the present moment, and put more thought and effort into each line of the song. This is good for technique, style and also for feeling self-conscious, as it takes away any feelings about past mistakes, or worries about future sections/ lyrics, etc.

1. Sing through a whole song, only allowing yourself to focus on 1 phrase at a time. For example: Looking out / on the morning rain, / I used to feel / so uninspired. Remember to focus on the pauses, as well.

2. How did you find this made you sing differently?

Notes from Step 3: Develop Your Technique

Step 4: Hone Your Style

I used to be self-conscious about the fact that I didn't feel like I had my own singing style. What didn't occur to me at the time was that I simply needed to work on it and develop it - like everything else!

Emphasis on Artistry

Once we have a technical foundation, we can focus on our artistry and honing the sounds and styles of singing that we like. Of course, the two go hand in hand and you will likely be discovering your own singing/musical style while also training your voice. A healthy balance between these two is key.

" Artistry is about being authentic. The value of technique is to serve your artistry, to allow you to be free and expressive. Perfectionism kills authenticity." - Wendy Parr, Holistic Vocal Coach

We can use technique as the tool to help us tune our instrument. Then, we need to learn how to play, and then we need to actually *play* (I mean that in the fun sense). We want to let the technique be present in the back of our minds, stored away in our cognitive brain. I say this because one thing we definitely want to avoid is perfectionism. I have seen many times when singers have focused purely on technique and their artistry has suffered as a result. Our perfectionist brain, fuelled by our limiting self-beliefs loves for us to be obsessed with getting the perfect sound, or simply trapped in not being able to "let go" for fear of making mistakes. In order to play around and discover our own style, and the elements of singing and musical expression we like, we must not be afraid of making mistakes. We will practice this in the next chapter.

So, what is "style", anyway? Well, in a nut shell, it is the ways you choose to express yourself. It is all the little mannerisms and doing things in a particular way, that are unique to you. Style can take a long time to form consistently and comes from a collection of many things you like. In singing, one's style could take the form of tone (gravelly, smooth, breathy, clear), dynamics (soft, loud), rhythmical phrasing, use of melissma (runs, trills), use of twang, improvising, emotional connection, facial expression, warmth, and many more possibilities I have likely not thought of.

I've often been asked by singers, "What style of music suits my voice?" When asked this question, I like to simply pose questions back to the student: "What type of music do you listen to? What singers inspire you the most? What type of music did you grow up listening to?" It truly is not for me to say, because there is so much more to developing style and artistry than how a voice sounds. And anyway, to give my opinion on this would generalise style and pigeon hole a singer into a box, i.e. "People with heavy voices must sing soul" or "You've got a gravelly voice, so that means you must sing blues."

Beware of Being Taught Style

To teach style would be the same as putting words into someone's mouth, and not only that, it is stifling and detrimental to genres of music as a whole, potentially stalling their growth and movement forward into fresh new areas. Examples of this are genre stereotypes like: "All rock artists sing with grit in their voice", "All soul singers do runs and trills", or "All country singers use 'twang'..." etc.

We must allow ourselves to develop our own sense of musical styling, and this comes from a combination of our musical interests, our previous exposure to music (think of Aretha Franklin growing up in Gospel communities) and the sound we wish to portray to the world. This is to allow true creativity and the creation of true art. Exciting, fresh, never-heard-before sound can develop from finding our own true singing style. We must not manufacture robotic pop stars who are clones of previous singers.

Although, as I'm writing this, I'm remembering that part of my own journey as a singer was copying the artists I loved. There were a couple of years in my early twenties when I was obsessed with Eva Cassidy. I listened to her album Live at Blues Alley and sang along and felt free for the first time. (In fact, during this phase I realised I was actually pretty depressed. This album helped me express what was buried deep inside.) The problem was, when I sang Eva's songs in public, I styled them the exact way she did. I felt like I didn't have any elements that I could use in my own repertoire, so I just copied hers. Once my eyes were opened to this from my singing teacher, Leon, pointing it out to me, I felt like a total fraud. This was nothing more than glorified karaoke.

Borrowing From (Not Copying) the Singers we Love

A big part of finding your own style is developing a collection of some of the little elements and nuances we love from other artists and musical styles. That is why you can hear Billie Holiday in Amy Winehouse's style and Barbra Streisand in Lady Gaga's style. Leading Vocal Coach John Henny says, "There is a huge difference between being influenced (by your favourite artist) and copying", and that we must develop "deep listening skills" in order to pick up on all the beautiful nuances and exciting variations and possibilities in singing. Variations in phrasing, rhythm, subtleties in colour, vowel shaping, onsets of notes, and length of sustaining notes are some examples of elements we can experience by singing along with singers so that we can learn to have more depth and interest in our own singing.

John says we will naturally be drawn to certain qualities and the key is having a varied collection that will ultimately become our own style, so that we sing *'like'* our favourite singers, but we do not try to sound exactly like one particular artist.

❝ Try and pick up what they are doing with the phrasing. When they hesitate – why do they hesitate? Are they building tension, or anticipation? It's just a beautiful thing to hear. You can allow your own creativity to grow out of their exampling." (Henny, The Intelligent Vocalist Podcast, 2020)

So, how to do you even stop copying? Well, awareness that you are doing it is the first step. Then, it is also wise to aim to sing completely straight, without any styling at all: no slides, no dynamic changes from soft to loud, no runs/trills/fills, etc. This, by the way, can be quite difficult, so stick with it, go slow and be patient. And know that this is going to feel very boring and perhaps robotic. But it is important to be able to strip singing back to basics so that we can get out of the habit of copying. Then, we can start to add our own artistic choices.

After singing with little to no styling, what you can do is pinpoint a variety of stylistic elements you like in other singers, piece them together and incorporate them into your own singing with a lot of practice on *varying* songs. Then, you will naturally start to phrase lyrics, create tone and use dynamic and rhythmic changes in a way that is unique to you (with elements of the styles that have influenced you along the way).

★ Listening Exercise:

I often say in lessons "Great singers make the strangest noises". If we stop for a minute and think about how it would feel on the inside to make these kinds of sounds, it helps us to not feel silly/embarrassed/exposed when we do more of this ourselves. Listening carefully is also a great way to pinpoint which aspects in singing/music that we love.

Play these songs and focus on the prompts while you listen:

1. **Sia's EP Zero 7, track 'Destiny' or 'Somersault'** - The lyric phrasing, the vocal fry, the quiver in her voice, the moving from breathy to edgy, and the use of melisma.

2. **Nina Simone 'I Put a Spell on You'** – The emphasis on the word 'spell' in the first line, her clipped phrasing, the frantic energy in her vocal, and the use of scat sounds.

3. **Kate Bush 'Wuthering Heights'** – Singing constantly in this upper range (wailing), and her diction on the lyrics.

4. **Prince 'When Doves Cry'** – The opening sounds, the use of vocal fry, the syncopated rhythm of the lyric delivery, and the use of falsetto.

5. **Kurt Cobain on Nirvana's 'About a Girl'** – Gravelly singing, being on the edge of the vocal break, and using that cracking in the delivery.

6. **Corey Taylor from Slipknot 'Psychosocial'** – The song starts with a death metal 'scream'. (Side note: Fans of hardcore are drawn to this primal sound because it sounds so raw and emotional. However, if done incorrectly, it can wreak havoc on the voice. We can learn to vocalise in this way so that it doesn't actually put too much stress on the voice. There are techniques for this.)

7. **Freddie Mercury 'Bohemian Rhapsody'** – The in and out of falsetto, the full chest with grit, the smooth mix, and the holding notes long and fluidly, often applying breathiness.

There are literally thousands of examples. Which singers do you like and why?

| Exercise: Collecting and Applying Styles You Love |

1. Think of the main singers you love. What is it exactly about their singing that you like? Be as detailed as possible and list out on paper what it is you like. ie. 1. I love the different changing vocal dynamics that Eva Cassidy uses – very soft and breathy on one word/phrase then strong and edgy on the next. 2. I like the 'rockabilly' quiver in Freddy Mercury's voice on "This Thing Called Love". 3. I love the gentle way Billie Eilish draws out finishing her words to the very last second before moving on to the next word.

2. Now, try mimicking these vocal concepts yourself, and this part is key: *on other songs.* Do not copy those elements on the original songs (or even songs by that artist). Try incorporating these elements into totally different songs. Pick 5 songs to start with and start singing them, aiming to add these vocal elements you have discovered.

3. Print out the lyrics. Change it up: use a different stylistic choice or technique for each phrase or line and notate it on your lyrics. This is not set in stone; it just acts as a visual guide to start with. As you practice, it will start to come naturally to you, which aspect to add and when, and you will start to develop new ones!

Having a Repertoire

If you are a gigging singer, you will have a developed repertoire of songs that you have rehearsed in and out. So, it is this repetition of singing the same songs over and over again that dulls the other feelings that may arise before/ during a performance. When we perform, our brains are multi-tasking so many things, so the fewer new elements your brain has to process, the more at ease you will feel.

❝ I was terrified, which is generally a good reason to go through with something." – Natalie Portman

Many singers get a lot of anxiety around talking at a performance when introducing their songs and talking to the audience between songs. This is not that different from the actual song material and can be rehearsed beforehand. Doing so does not make your performance too staged, or un-authentic; it simply gives you more options to pull from. You can still remain in the moment and responsive to what is going on around you. Don't treat it as a script, as such, but a prompt, should you need it.

Quite simply, the more prepared you are before a performance, the less likely it is that something will go wrong.

| Exercise: Gathering Your Repertoire |

Sometimes it all looks so easy that it can seem like performers simply turn up and sing out of the blue, but we don't see all the work and preparation that has led up to that moment. Every performer has a selection of songs that they know well and have rehearsed many times over, which is why it looks so easy.

For this exercise, you will need a folder with clear inserts.

1. Pick out 5–10 songs that you know and love and that represent you as a singer and what you want to express. You might want to group genres together and do this exercise for each different genre, such as pop, jazz, soul, etc.

2. Print out the lyrics and sheet music if you will be singing with a band. The sheet music should be in the right key for your voice.

Note: to see if a song is in the right key, you'll need to know the lowest notes and the highest notes of the song in that key. Check to see how it feels and sounds. If you are unsure how to transpose music into a new key, it is a great idea to learn, but for now, there are several websites that transpose charts or scores for you, such as tabs.ultimate-guitar.com, or musicnotes.com.

3. Place your song sheets (with 2/3 copies of the music charts if applicable for live musicians) in the clear inserts. You can also store your notes on technique and paraphrasing the lyrics, etc., in these folders.

Now you have a repertoire book! Add to this as you gain new material. Practice your songs until you know them inside and out. You may want to change up the same songs, too – ballad to up-tempo and vice-versa, different styling techniques, etc.

| Exercise: Practicing Your Performance Chat |

It's important to rehearse all parts of our performance, even the chit chat before and in the middle of songs. Remember that it is okay to be honest and open about feeling nervous or self-conscious – this will only make your audience love you even more!

What we are trying to do by rehearsing is to make sure we aren't repeating ourselves or saying something that doesn't flow quite right. For example, I remember seeing a gig once, and the singer said before every single song, "This song is about X, and I really hope you like it." Okay, so I realise this doesn't seem too bad, but it was just that she had the same script, and the same formula every single time! So, after the first few songs, it seemed pretty robotic.

Of course, even worse than repeating yourself is babbling on and on with no end in sight! We've all experienced that boring speech that never ends. You want to make sure you have a little chat to connect, but then bring it to a close and start the next number.

Here are three steps you can follow when planning your performance chat:

1.   Write down a formula of potential things to say, in case you get stuck or tempted to repeat yourself. For the sake of practicing expanding on this, use the following prompts to write some detail below about some of your material:

What the song is about

_____

Why you have chosen this song

_____

What this song means to you

_____

Why you sing/perform

What drew you to the genre of music you perform

You can also:

Introduce the band members
Say something about the venue or location

2. Sit or stand in a room as if you were on a stage, ready for a performance. Go through and talk to a pretend audience, rehearsing what you will say before and in between each song.

3. Set up your phone or computer so that you can record yourself doing this. Practice the performance chat on camera, then watch it back. What did you like or what didn't you like? Make some adjustments based on what you saw. Repeat this exercise as necessary – remember that the more you rehearse, the more confident you will feel and come across.

Notes from Step 4: Hone Your Style

Step 5: Play Around and Make Mistakes

Do you feel that somewhere along the way in your development, there have been times when you lost track of the enjoyment of singing and simply just being creative and messing around? This can easily happen when we start to focus on the outcome of our experiences, rather than the process. We so desire a certain outcome that we forget how to have fun and enjoy the ride in the meantime.

❝ You can only go forward by making mistakes." Alexander McQueen

We need to allow ourselves regular space to play around and make mistakes. Mistakes are a huge part of growth, not only because we can learn from them, but because without allowing ourselves to make mistakes, our perfectionist brain keeps us in "safe mode". When we don't take any risks in singing, it can result in a bland performance. No one wants that, right?

If you struggle with perfectionism or the need to get it just right (which is extremely common among artists), then that could signify that there is an underlying self-belief of feeling not good enough, that mistakes and failure are bad, and that stems from the fear of rejection.

Barns Courtney writes himself a large, visual note when he's song-writing that says "Write for the trash can". This reminds him to keep putting his art out there, to keep "shooting hoops", as he says, because no points will be scored if we just stand on the side-lines waiting to get everything perfectly lined up.

" Don't think about making art, just get it done. Let everyone else decide if it's good or bad, whether they love it or hate it. While they are deciding, make even more art." - Andy Warhol

| Exercise: Play time |

Literally set aside some time in your schedule for simply messing around. Set a timer, and within this time, there are no limits or rules on your singing. Simply give yourself permission to enjoy it and have fun! It can be transformative to literally book in your fun singing time every week, or even daily.

| Permission Slip |

To help with this process of making mistakes, I'd like you to sign a permission slip for yourself. Make sure to read the note out loud (very important).

| Exercise: Change up your approach |

To play around with your singing, literally aim to mess things up! There are no rules to pure creativity. Start by choosing one or two aspects from the following list to change when you sing, then choose another two:

○**Rhythm**: Come in late and then speed up to catch up with yourself. Play around with singing choppy/rhythmical or smooth/connected.

○**Melody**: Start by changing one or two notes in each phrase. Add runs/riffs or a different ending to a phrase.

○**Dynamics**: Loud vs. soft, edgy vs. breathy

○**Vowel shape**: Lengthen or widen the vowel to get the sound you desire.

○**Vibrato/No Vibrato**: Try holding a note straight before letting it resolve with vibrato.

○**Tone and Weight of voice**: Choosing a dark or bright tone, adding a gravelly voice, heavy or light in weight.

○**Lyrics**: Change up the lyrics to suit you.

○**Tempo**: Slow a fast song right down, or vice versa

○**Key**: Changing the key of a song can really change how it sits in your range and which parts of your voice are highlighted.

○**Genre**: Sing a grunge song in a jazz style, or change a country song to RnB, etc.

You will likely find that once you change one thing, a snowball effect happens and other changes start happening naturally. This is how we can really revive and freshen up singing that has become overly "safe".

I encourage you to do this with every song. Literally, never sing your songs the same way twice. Change it up depending on your mood and what is happening around you.

"Improvisation is the expression of the accumulated yearnings, dreams, and wisdom of the soul." – Yehudi Menuhin

Putting Emotion into Singing

Expressing emotion when singing comes more naturally to some than others. A song never conveys just one emotion; such as happy, sad, or mad; despite what people may think. There are a variety of nuances we can express when we sing. Like real life situations, we move freely from one emotional nuance to another, and it can be complex and messy. This can give a performance so much more depth and interest than if you focused on just one emotion.

See the following diagram of psychologist Robert Plutchik's Wheel of Emotions. You can see how many shades and nuances of emotions are possible to express in a performance.

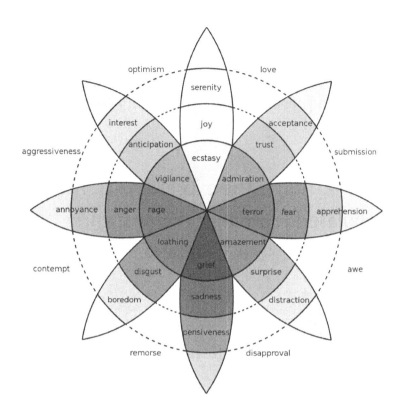

According to Plutchnik, humans experience eight different primary emotions, which grow in intensity as they move to the center of the wheel. The emotions can also be divided into 4 distinct pairs of polar opposites; joy/sadness, anticipation/surprise, fear/anger, and disgust/trust. In the middle of each emotion is a blend of the two on either side. For example, Plutchnik says serenity and acceptance can produce love.

For the sake of using this diagram for our singing practice, we can use it as a prompt to identify and then express the emotion which feels the most appropriate.

Each phrase of your song might have a different emotion, or progressing emotions such as we see on the wheel, i.e. pensiveness to sadness to grief.

Artistic development coach Wendy Parr says that if you are unsure which emotion to start with, choosing anger is a good way to access a feeling and let it blossom from there. Often, anger can bring out other, underlying emotions.

| Exercise: Feel It on the In-Breath |

We take a breath in, then speak and sing as we release the out breath. I like the analogy of a surfer, riding on the flow of the wave. Our breath is the wave that powers our speech or singing. The flow of our breath carries our voice, and it also carries our emotional intention for each line or phrase. For example, if you take a breath now and think of someone you really love, then when you go to sing or speak, your voice will be filled with love. This can hugely impact how you deliver your lyrics, and it is a powerful way to show real emotion and feelings in your singing.

For this exercise, it is best to go slow at first. It gets easier and faster the more we practice this. Think of the emotion you feel or want to express on certain lines/ phrases of your songs.

I like to take my song lyrics and mark out the main places I am going to take breaths. I write down the emotion I want to convey for the next phrase. As I'm singing, I then think about that emotion when I breathe in, in preparation for that line. As I release and sing, I let this feeling come through my singing. The results are sometimes astounding. It makes me sing completely different at times, improvising in ways that surprise me as I hear it coming out of my mouth. This is true expression of emotion.

| Exercise: Improvising the Melody |

For this exercise it is important to put the perfectionist brain to the side. Improvising is an important part of singing; it is true freedom and creativity, but in order to be open to it we need to feel okay about making mistakes. This exercise is an exploration and should be approached with a light heart. Although, it may take some time for some people to relax into this, and that's okay! Stick with it.

Repeat the exercise as often as you can, first with this song and then on your own chosen songs.

On the song 'What a Wonderful World' the chords are provided. If you don't know the song, start by learning the basic melody, and then we want to explore playing around with that – i.e. choosing alternative notes. Live accompaniment is best so that you can change up the rhythm and feel, but if that isn't possible, then a backing track may be used.

Aim to change some aspects in each line; this could be the melody, the rhythm, or the dynamics (breathy, soft, edgy, loud, etc). For the melody, go low when you are meant to go high and vice versa, adding melisma (movement on notes). Be brave! If you mess up, which will likely happen as you are exploring, don't worry! Your ear will naturally move your voice to a note that works with the music. These mistakes can often end up with some of the coolest changes that you would not have done otherwise.

It is well documented that many great songs and musical moment have occurred purely out of accidents!

"What a Wonderful World"
by Louis Armstrong

Verse:

    F   C   Dm   Am
I see trees of green, red roses too
Gm   F   A7   Dm
I see them bloom, for me and you,
    Bb   C   F
And I think to myself, What a wonderful
world.

Verse:

    F   C   Dm   Am
I see skies of blue and clouds of white,
Gm   F   A7   Dm
The bright blessed day, the dark sacred
night,
    Bb   C   F
And I think to myself, what a wonderful
world

Bridge:
    C   F
The colours of a rainbow are so pretty in
the sky

C   F
Are also on the faces of people going by
    Dm   Am   Dm   Am
I see friends shaking hands saying how do
you do
Dm   Am F   C
They're really saying I love you.

Verse:

```
      F     C     Dm             Am
I hear babies cry, I watch them grow
Gm                     F     A7            Dm
They'll learn much more than I'll ever know,
      Bb                C                 F
And I think to myself what a wonderful world


      Bb                C                 F
Yes I think to myself, what a wonderful
world.
```

Notes from Step 5: Play Around and Make Mistakes

Section 3: Focus Outward

(Steps 6, 7 &8)

Step 6: Turn Your Focus Externally

When we are experiencing self-consciousness, we are focussed internally. What if we could simply choose to turn our focus externally? We can, with the right preparation, tools and awareness. In order to do that, let's first look at a key point: The fact that everyone around you is actually only concerned with themselves.

Great News: It's Not About You

The concept I'm going to discuss now marked a huge turning point for me in my development as a confident singer. When I heard and then finally understood this vital point, then I really "got it". "It" refers to why we as humans enjoy music so much. It's why the hairs on our arms stand on end when we hear a beautiful singing voice. It's why certain lyrics combined with a tone of voice can bring tears to our eyes.

In a nutshell: We enjoy hearing someone sing because of the way it makes *US* feel. We aren't thinking about how the performer feels!

Let's look at the lead up to a performance through the eyes of some people in the room.

When you are the *performer* you may experience hundreds of thoughts and emotions racing in your brain. Some of these might include:

•Worry about if everyone in the audience will enjoy your singing
•Worry about people in the audience judging you
•Worry about your technique (or lack of)
•Worry about how your voice sounds on certain notes
•General anxiety/anticipation
•Worry about not coming in at the right time
•Worry that you won't be in tune
•Worry that the audience will feel you're a "faker"
•Worry about forgetting lyrics
•Worry about how you look
•What to do with your hands
•Wanting to give a great (energetic, emotional, dynamic, etc. etc.) performance

❝ I couldn't let myself completely go when I sang because I had a fear about showing my facial expressions in that moment." – Barns Courtney

When you are the *sound engineer* for a performance, you might be having these thoughts:

•Worry/anticipation of getting set up on time
•Worry about using new equipment/set up in a new setting
•Worry about the microphones or speakers feeding back during the performance
•Worry about remembering the levels/setup for different songs

When you are in the *audience* of a performance, you might be having these thoughts:

•Excitement about having a great time
•Enjoyment of being out at an event
•Enjoyment of being sociable
•Anticipation about whether or not the show will be good

So, the point of listing out all of these potential thoughts is to demonstrate that each experience is in the eye of the beholder.

The thought that transformed my whole view on singing was: "IT IS NOT ABOUT ME. IT IS ABOUT HOW I MAKE THEM FEEL."

In fact, it could be said that *the very responsibility* of a performer is to create a mood for the listener, to make them feel a certain way. That could be sad, happy, elated, excited, angry or reflective. Audience members do not care how the performer is feeling, or if they are anxious. They just want to be entertained or they simply want to enjoy the music.

There will undoubtedly be some element of judgement from audience members. It is a performance, after all. That is why there are stage lights and a production is made out of a show. Many people may judge performers on what they are wearing, what they sound like and what statement they may be making. *But the important thing to remember is that the performer doesn't have any control over this.*

In fact, there are only two things we can control in this world: our own thoughts and our own actions.

So, truly, what is the point in stressing over what people think about us? They will be living in their own little world, feeling how you make THEM feel as you sing. In fact, we really only get the present moment we are in to make an impact. After the performance, the listeners may remember, but it will be a dulled down memory, as life will continue with their normal lives and they will go on to feel new feelings and have new experiences. We may stress continually over every last mistake, but truly, no one else will care or remember.

| Exercise: Smiling in Performance |

The simple act of smiling is so powerful. It instantly puts your audience at ease and can help yourself feel so much better, too. When you smile as you sing, it looks to your audience as if you are having the time of your life – and that is exactly how it should look! The only exception is if you are singing a song with dark emotions attached to it. However, you might still smile as you are introducing the song.

I often notice singers performing or people speaking on camera not smiling enough. Not smiling is one of the biggest tell-tale signs that we are feeling nervous or self-conscious. By smiling, you make your audience feel comfortable, and it will even trick your own mind into thinking that everything is okay. It can also help bring you out of a negative headspace.

Try this:

1.   Smile while looking into a mirror, and notice how many different types of smiles you can do. (Cheesy grin, natural smile with teeth, smile with no teeth, laughing smile, shy smile, humble smile, etc.)

2. Sing a song while looking at yourself in the mirror. Make sure to smile naturally at regular key points throughout your whole performance.

What did you notice? What areas could you improve? Do you need to make it more natural? Did you drop the smiling after the first few notes?

| Exercise: Singing Outside |

Find a quiet space *outside* where you are totally alone. This may be tricky if you live in a city! Choose an odd hour, or an odd part of town where you have space (make sure you are safe!). Sing a song, out loud!

If you feel obliged, video yourself doing this and post it in our supportive Facebook group, "Singing for Myself".

Acting as a Tool for Singers

There is so much we can learn about letting go from acting, and acting within a song can help us to dull down the sensation of "baring our soul", as we are essentially taking on a role. Great acting really is portraying "the truth" as you intend the truth to be in every line or phrase, or even every pause in your performance. It is NOT being over the top or making big gestures. Acting can be very subtle and very natural. Acting can serve us as another tool to "hold onto" and distract us from any negative whirring thoughts happening internally

Different levels of self-consciousness affect behaviour, as it is common for people to act differently when they "lose themselves in a crowd". Being in a crowd, being in a dark room, or wearing a disguise creates anonymity and temporarily decreases self-consciousness. [1]

I have noticed that actors do not seem to have this problem of feeling self-conscious. Well, at least they don't appear to be feeling self-conscious in any way. And if they do seem self-conscious, then they are outwardly showing this in an intentional way, as part of the role they have taken on. In fact, with acting, everything seems to be done intentionally, and the performer is always connected in each moment and always presenting "outward".

❝ You're less likely to let nerves take over if you're engaged in the image, the fantasy, and the moment. In fact, if your nerves get the best of you, instead of feeling as if you are standing there being judged, think of making your performance more expressive, more connected to your imagery." – Rhonda Carlson, "What Do I Do with My Hands?"

Playing a Role Authentically

How do actors discover, connect to and then perform as their roles? Anne Leatherland is a Specialist Voice Trainer with many years' experience teaching in Musical Theatre. She says that, firstly, actors *inhabit* the roles they play. It isn't something they simply put on; they literally inhabit everything about the character. In other words, they seem to become the characters – no longer actors reciting their lines. It is as if they live the lives of their characters. This would mean taking a step back and looking at your material through a totally different lens. And in the case of singing contemporary music, each song will likely be a different character, or from a different view point. Are you singing in first person, or are you the story teller?

Anne says that playing a role authentically is all about drawing context from our own situations: this is how we can have believable performances without over-acted clichés. Look at the character's situation and find the connection and overlaps with yourself. How would you respond in their situation? Another good explanation of taking on a role in this way is "real living in imaginary circumstances" (Meisner) so that we can "be alive emotionally" within a performance. (Brunetti 2007).

Have you noticed the full circle happening here, in relation to the subject matter of this book? We can use acting as a tool to down our feelings of self-consciousness; however, when we act, we must pull from our own personal experiences in order for it to be authentic and truthful.

Adding Depth and Context

Let's look at practical ways we can delve into our material further for engaging, truthful performances that come to life. The book 'What Do I Do with my Hands?' by Rhonda Carlson shows us how we can determine the WHO, the WHAT and the WHERE & WHEN that apply to your song.

WHO: Who is it that you are singing to, or singing about? If you are singing a love song, is it to your partner, or perhaps your mother? Or maybe to your best friend, a beloved pet, or even yourself.

WHAT: What are the details of the situation? Perhaps you are singing to your best friend who moved away a long time ago, and you never felt the same with another friend since. Perhaps you are singing about your mother and you are angry and hurt that she let you down by talking about you to your sister behind your back.

WHERE & WHEN: Create a scenario for your song. Use your senses to recall certain situations from your past: a chill in the air and a sense of anticipation on the first day of school, the smell of cinnamon coming from your grandmother's kitchen during the holidays, a waft of cigarette smoke on the coat of the mysterious person you met in a bar.

If your song just doesn't seem to evoke any feelings or memories you can draw from, you can imagine a scenario or you can SUBSTITUTE feelings, actions and behaviours from particular times in your life. Say, if you want your performance to come across as vulnerable, you might borrow aspects of your personality/behaviour from a time or particular instance when you felt that way.

" What is their (in reference to character acting) desire? Desire is at the heart of everything." – Natalie Portman

The more detailed your scenarios are, the more depth your acting and gestures will have. This makes our performance more believable, because this is how we actually are in real life. Rhonda demonstrates this by asking, "What would be the first thing you do if you found out you won the lottery? Perhaps your first thought is that you would jump up and down and scream, but actually, what really might happen would be a surprised thought of,

"Who, me?" and then, "Surely this is a mistake," and, "Did I even play those same numbers this week?" before finally jumping and screaming.

Going into such detail with your material will not only give your performance a new life, it will certainly distract from any negative, self-conscious chatter happening internally. In fact, now that you have all of this newfound information and ways to express your singing, there isn't likely going to be any room left over for self-conscious thoughts!

Avoiding Clichés

Rhonda also warns about avoiding the common "hand out" gesture that many singers use when acting their lyrics. In reality, we really don't see anyone do this motion unless they are asking for spare change. The other common movement singers often do is place their clasped hands on their stomach, which also isn't a natural action in real life unless we are ill. Instead, we must simply let our natural reactions and instincts guide our actions in response to the lyrics we sing, and the meaning/stories we associate with them.

| Exercise: Strong Stance |

Adopting a strong and open pose, like a superhero, can actually help us to feel more confident. It's true! Numerous psychological studies have shown that if we stand in a strong pose, then we feel that we have more power, whereas if we stand in a closed pose, then we are more likely to feel powerless.

Practice standing with legs slightly apart, hands on hips and chest open. Stay there for several minutes with your head held high. Then practice walking into a room in a relaxed, calm manner (don't forget to breathe), and take your place where you will sing.

How do you feel?

| Exercise: Practicing Acting Within Your Material |

1. Decide who the character you are portraying is for the songs in your repetoire. Get to know these characters. What are they like? What are they going through? How are they similar to you?

2. Decide the WHO, WHAT, WHERE & WHEN for each of the songs in your repertoire. You might want to print out

your lyrics and write details about the stories in the margins.

3. Now practice singing them, focusing on inhabiting the characters and telling the stories.

What did you notice about singing in this way? What would you change? What would you keep?

| Exercise: Acting 'As If' |

1. Think about a singer or performer that you admire. It might be someone who oozes confidence on stage or has a natural ability to make their audience feel at ease. Write down what it is about this person's performance that you like.

1. Now picture inside your mind what it might feel like as you are applying those same concepts. Actually, visualise yourself singing through your own material and acting in the same manner as the performer you admire.

1. Now sing through some material. Act "as if" you are just like this person. Do this, even though you may not feel that way.

Note: You are not pretending you are the same person; you are embodying their traits into your own performance.

How did this make you feel? How did it affect your performance?

Notes from Step 6: Focus Outward

Step 7: Observe Yourself

The practice of being outwardly focussed needs to be solidified with some self-awareness and acceptance of reality. If we don't know what we look or sound like, then this unknown will always be looming above our heads, waiting to pounce in the form of self-consciousness. Whereas, if we already have an awareness about how we look or sound to others, then we will feel more in control. I'm sure you have had the experience of suddenly hearing your voice or seeing yourself on camera and feeling rather, well, odd. The more you can get used to seeing/hearing yourself from the 3rd person, the more we can line up our internal sense of self with our outwardly actions.

I have practiced this step a lot in the writing of this book and online course. I have taken video of myself talking on camera. It's been a huge step in my development and has really helped me to be more of a natural "performer", while at the same time, shutting off my overly self-conscious thoughts.

This step is all about the doing, rather than the theory, which is why it appears shorter at first. You will be amazed at the revelations you have when you start watching yourself back. You will find many things that you may be unaware of: habits and mannerisms such as using your hands to guide your for notes, sliding up to pitches, how much energy you put across, how comfortable you seem, the sound of your high notes in your head vs. in the recording, and much more.

Spend a lot of time here, and be kind to yourself. Aim to merely observe first, then pin point the areas you want change, go back and do it again. All the while, the act of recording and watching yourself over and over again will be helping you get more comfortable turning your focus outward.

| Exercise: Recording Yourself and Watching Back |

1.Set up your phone or computer to record yourself singing.

2.Record yourself doing the exercises from Step 6: Smiling on Stage, Practicing Acting Within Your Material, and Acting "As If".

3.Watch back your performances and make note of what you liked about your singing/performance, and what you didn't.

4.Repeat the recording process and watch back now, with any/all of the songs in your repertoire, making note of what you like and what you don't like.

5.Repeat the exercise, aiming to improve on the areas you want to change.

| Exercise: Post Yourself Singing in Our Group |

Record yourself singing a song of your choice and upload it to our supportive 'Singing for Myself' private Facebook Page!

Notes from Step 7: Observe Yourself

Step 8: Take Small & Regular Action Steps

From the past 20 years coaching students of all levels, I have noticed the most profound improvements in the students who take regular, small steps forward. The great news is that to take small steps every day is much easier, and less scary, than trying to take huge leaps. In fact, this is exactly how I wrote this book. I had the idea growing for many years, but I got the urge to start writing and forming this into a book during the COVID-19 lockdown in 2020. Every day, my husband and I swopped places from home-schooling duties in the afternoon, and I quietly chipped away for 2 hours most days. One day, in utter amazement, I realised that the first draft of the book was completed.

Looking back over my own career, I realise now that the self-consciousness I have experienced is down to lack of examination and exercise in certain areas, including aspects of my mindset and singing skill sets that I needed to hone, adjust and practice. In my own mind, it felt much bigger than this - kind of like a huge barrier or hurdle that I could never get across. I'm not trying to belittle anyone's experience with these feelings. I know for some it is more severe than others, and sometimes it does come from having a heightened sensitive side (which, remember, is a positive trait, not negative or weak, like sensitivity is often portrayed to be). But the point is, we can uncover the reasons why we are held back by our self-conscious side and then take steps to do something about it. Then we work through it, and then we get over it.

What we are going to do now is look at the specific areas that you might be feeling self-conscious about. This is likely a sign that you need to address some issues and do something about them.

Let's look back at the mindfulness exercise in Step 2 where you wrote down all the worries you have about performing. Now take your list, and cross out the worries that are simply not really your problem, such as worrying what the audience will think about you. Are you left with some worries that might have a bit more substance?

Same idea for the exercise in Step 1 when you wrote down those "mean thoughts' that came to you as you sang out loud. Which of these mean thoughts just stem from unreasonable fears, and which of them might have an element of truth, in that you could be self-conscious for a reason that you can address?

★Action Step: Highlight Your Improvement Goals

Make a list of the areas you want to improve on in your singing/performing. Give yourself a timeline and a goal for each of these areas. For example: I want to better accompany myself singing some jazz standards on piano (playing a walking bassline in the left and comping in my right hand), and to sing 5 songs in my repertoire. My goal is to showcase them on Facebook Live on my Becky Gilhespie Vocal Coach page, and I'm going to put that in my diary for 6 months' time.

If your problem area has to do with technique, hire a coach to improve. If it has to do with not having any performance opportunities, find an open mic or a singing group, etc.

"What small step do you need to take today in order to get closer to your goal?" – Line Hilton, Vocal Performance and Resilience Coach

| Exercise: Exposing Your Home Truths|

Here, we are going to need that trustworthy person in your life again.

1.   Sing a song, or part of a song, in front of this person with whom you feel comfortable, and with whom you can speak honestly and openly.

2.   Just afterwards, have a frank and open conversation about what he/she did or did not like about your performance. You may gain some insight into areas that need improvement from another perspective.

What was the outcome? Are there things you need to address and work on?

How Will You Respond to Negative Results?

Let's face it, it is likely that you may come up against some hard truths and/or negative feedback, or potentially make a big mistake, or find yourself in an embarrassing scenario. This is truly part of being human. How will you process this? Be prepared that this may validate some underlying negative beliefs, such as "I'm a failure" or "I've been rejected". Remember, though, that you can choose how to interpret this instance. Make sure to explore the different possible interpretations, like we did in the Alternative Interpretation exercise from Step 2.

What we can do is make sure we are in a *growth mindset*, whereby we choose to see this feedback as purely data, with which we can go back to the drawing-room, tweak things as necessary and emerge again.

J.K. Rowling was rejected by 12 publishers before one picked up 'Harry Potter', and the Wright Brothers were only able to create a successful airplane because of all their previous failed attempts. Studies show that those who fail regularly and keep trying anyway are better equipped to respond to challenges and setbacks.

★ Action Step: Get Out of Your Mind and Into Your Body

This one actually involves physical exercise. Exercise can yield amazing results in feeling good, as a jolt of moderate cardiovascular exercise releases dopamine into the brain. Whenever I am prone to feeling a little overly self-conscious, I simply go for a run or join a class in the morning. It literally sets up my day with more confidence and positivity. It also helps me to release any stored tension. I urge you to try exercise – enough cardiovascular energy to get your blood pumping through your body, such as jogging, dancing, skipping, stepping, etc. This is a great thing to do on days when you might have an actual performance, because it will help release any tension and increase your confidence and positive feelings.

★ Action Step: Say Yes

In order to move forward and truly kick our self-consciousness to the curb, we must be singing in front of others on a regular basis. Make a conscious decision to seek out and then say YES to any singing opportunities that come your way. Don't overthink it. Don't focus on how it will happen; just say yes. You will find a way to make it happen.

Useful and Practical Strategies for Overcoming Self-Consciousness

○Be in the moment
○Focus on what you are doing (being a messenger of a song/lyrics/feeling/expression)
○Focus on the process, not the outcome
○Have fun with it
○Sing more
○Focus on your actions
○Commit to a "Growth Mindset"
○Express gratitude often
○Get rid of "mean thoughts"
○Journal your thoughts and worries
○Meditate and breathe
○Make strange noises and faces, regularly
○Look in the mirror as you sing
○Video yourself
○Sing in front of a trusted friend
○Sing outside in the open air
○Have a solid technique
○Acquire a sense of your own style
○Express your feelings when you sing
○Breathe in with a feeling, then let that feeling go on the out breath
○Have a practiced repertoire
○Paraphrase your lyrics
○Inhabit the character in your songs
○Determine the WHO, WHAT, WHEN & WHERE of your songs' storylines

○Work on your natural gestures
○Act 'as if' when performing
○Smile or laugh at regular points through performance
○Uncover and work on any issues in your voice
○Say "yes" to opportunities before thinking "no"
○Undertake physical exercise often

Your Very First Strategy

Feelings of self-consciousness can come on fast and strong, and it can seem like there is nowhere to escape. Personally, I feel the easiest and quickest thing you can do is simply to smile and/or laugh right away, as soon as you experience a self-conscious moment. This makes both you and your audience feel at ease, lightens the situation and has an endearing quality. And this will naturally snowball into more positive experiences.

The Greatest Gift You Bring to the World

I will always remember how a fellow singing teacher and lovely friend of mine Laura Long got wind of the fact that I was shying away from my singing and holding back. She confronted me several times, reminding me that I have a talent for this - so why would I be letting it go to waste? I went on to have some lessons with her, and we explored some healing work together. She helped me to express myself through the songs that I chose that had meaning to me. I had never done that before. At first, I found myself (ugly) crying through singing - it was hard to get anything out. After releasing the emotion, I felt better so we paraphrased lyrics, applied emotion, and dynamic changes to reflect my feelings. I spent time playing around – giving myself permission to make mistakes and purely express myself through my songs. It was liberating. I will never forget that experience and I feel very grateful.

I would say the exact same to you. You have a calling for music and expressing yourself through singing. You have a voice like no other person in the world, and what is in your head is a collection of all your rich life experiences and observations that no one else can bring to the table in the same way that you can. The world needs to hear you.

Music is a healer of pain, a connector of people, a facilitator of creativity, a liberator of tension and an initiator of joy. You can choose to cast fear aside and let your voice be heard.

YOU are your greatest gift to the world.

Notes from Step 8: Take Regular Small Action Steps

Going Forward

Thank you for purchasing this book/program and following these steps. By doing so, you have made a commitment to proactively improve your singing experience. This will, in turn, affect the steps and decisions you make going forward. Please keep in touch in our supportive Facebook Group, 'Singing for Myself', to celebrate your wins and to connect with a group of like-minded singers.

I'm here for you: please get in touch if I can help you further with your development through private vocal lessons, or if you have a particular need and I can't help you myself, I likely know someone who can, and I can refer you.

You can return to any of the steps in this book whenever you feel you need to work on a certain area. I'm excited for you!

Email: vocals@beckygilhespie.com
Facebook group: 'Singing for Myself'
Facebook page: Becky Gilhespie Vocal Coach
Instagram: @beckygilhespievocalcoach
Website: vocals.beckygilhespie.com

➡ If you liked this book and found it helpful, please kindly give it a review on Amazon. This will help others find it.

About the Author

Becky Gilhespie (BBA, PGCE) is an International Vocal Coach. Originally from the US, she lived in London for 15 years where she studied Speech Level Singing with top teachers worldwide, including founder Seth Riggs (Michael Jackson, Barbra Streisand, Evanescence and more).

Becky now keeps up to date with the latest in vocal science and mindset training and strives to bring this to her own studio. She trains students online around the world and lives in the countryside in Berry, NSW, Australia. Becky loves singing jazz and cooking: she was a semi-finalist on UK Masterchef.

References:

[1] LAING, R.D. (1960) THE DIVIDED SELF: AN EXISTENTIAL STUDY IN SANITY AND MADNESS. HARMONDSWORTH: PENGUIN HTTPS://EN.WIKIPEDIA.ORG/WIKI/SELF-CONSCIOUSNESS

[2] PALL, C. 2016 POWER TOOL: SELF-AWARENESS VS. SELF-CONSCIOUSNESS: <HTTPS://COACHCAMPUS.COM/COACH-PORTFOLIOS/POWER-TOOLS/CORINA-PALL-SELF-AWARENESS-VS-SELF-CONSCIOUSNESS/>

[3]INNERJAM. 2020 THE POWER OF THE SUBCONSCIOUS MIND: CAN YOU CONTROL THE UNCONSCIOUS? HTTPS://INNERJAM.COM/SUBCONSCIOUS-MIND-POWER/

[4]_ ACADEMY OF IDEAS. 2018 PERFORMING THERAPY ON YOURSELF: SELF KNOWLEDGE AND SELF REALIZATION HTTPS://ACADEMYOFIDEAS.COM/2018/09/PERFORMING-THERAPY-ON-YOURSELF/

[5]_ HORNEY, K. 1951 NEUROSIS AND HUMAN GROWTH: THE STRUGGLE TOWARDS SELF REALIZATION W. W. NORTON & COMPANY; 2ND EDITION (MAY 18, 1991)

[6]_BROWN, B (2018) DARE TO LEAD. RANDOM HOUSE, 1ST EDITION.

[7]_IDEAPOD (2019) IMAGE: FIXED VS. GROWTH: THE TWO BASIC MINDSETS THAT SHAPE OUR LIVES HTTPS://IDEAPOD.COM/FIXED-VS-GROWTH-THE-TWO-BASIC-MINDSETS-THAT-SHAPE-OUR-LIVES/

[8]]_ HILTON, L. 2020 GETTING OVER IT SERIES EPISODE 3: THE GOOD, BAD AND THE UGLY OF ANXIETY <HTTPS://WWW.YOUTUBE.COM/WATCH?V=4Y_8H6VRJWA&FEATURE=YOUTU.BE&__S=EZM1Q011C4O2S1PXXVSH>

[9]]_ T.S. SATHYANARAYANA RAO, M. R. ASHA,1 K. S. JAGANNATHA RAO,2 AND P. VASUDEVARAJU2 2009 THE BIOCHEMISTRY OF BELIEF INDIAN J PSYCHIATRY; 51(4): 239–241

[10] METIVIER, A. 2020 TWO EASILY REMEMBERED QUESTIONS THAT SILENCE NEGATIVE THOUGHTS TEDX DOCKLANDS HTTPS://WWW.YOUTUBE.COM/WATCH?V=KVTYJDRISPM

[11]_ PERCY, L. 2015 MOTHER OM LEONIE PERCY; AMAZON AUSTRALIA SERVICES INC. 1ST EDITION

[12] TREINKMAN, MELISSA 2020: FOCUS OF ATTENTION IN VOICE TRAINING HTTPS://WWW.YOUTUBE.COM/WATCH? V=TPJBQDB9Y0M&FEATURE=YOUTU.BE

[13]]HENNY, JOHN 2020: SING LIKE, DON'T SOUND LIKE. THE INTELLIGENT VOCALIST PODCAST. HTTPS://JOHNHENNY.COM/ 181-2/

[14] ROBERT PLUTCHIK: WHEEL OF EMOTIONS.]HTTPS:// SIMPLE.WIKIPEDIA.ORG/WIKI/ROBERT_PLUTCHIK

[15] CARLSON, R. 2015 WHAT DO I DO WITH MY HANDS? PERSONAL DYNAMICS PUBLISHING; 2ND EDITION

[16]] PSYCHOLOGY TODAY 2007: WHY YOU MAY WANT TO STAND LIKE A SUPERHEROSUPERHERO HTTPS:// WWW.PSYCHOLOGYTODAY.COM/AU/BLOG/THE-SUPERHEROES/ 201107/WHY-YOU-MAY-WANT-STAND-SUPERHERO

[17] SKILS YOU NEED. 2020 THE IMPORTANCE OF MINDSET]HTTPS://WWW.SKILLSYOUNEED.COM/PS/ MINDSETS.HTML

[18] VOICE SCIENCE WORKS. RESONANCE HTTPS:// WWW.VOICESCIENCEWORKS.ORG/RESONANCE.HTML

[19] FINKLE, D. 2007: VOCAL EASE: ACTING WHILE SINGING BACKSTAGE MAGAZINE HTTPS://WWW.BACKSTAGE.COM/ MAGAZINE/ARTICLE/VOCAL-EASE-ACTING-SINGING-46768/